'SHUA

STORY BY WILLIAM BURKE
DRAWINGS BY MARY SOUTHARD, CSJ

ACTA Publications

Rev. William Burke is the associate pastor of Our Lady of Loretto Church in Hometown, Illinois.

Sr. Mary Southard, CSJ, is the co-director of Spiritearth in Dover, Massachusetts.

A video and an audio tape of Fr. Burke's performance of *'Shua* are available from ACTA Publications, 800-397-2282.

Editor: Gregory F. Augustine Pierce

Design: John Dylong

Typesetting: Link Book Development and Production

ISBN: 0-87946-052-0

Library of Congress Catalogue No.: 90-085661

Printed in the United States of America

Jesus grew
in wisdom,
age and
grace . . .

Luke 2:52

Prologue

Not long ago, I spent several months in Israel. One day, some friends and I were on the shore of Capernaum on the northern end of the Sea of Galilee. Our guide pointed over to the west to a break in the hills and said, "You see that? That's the Valley of the Doves. That's the way Jesus would have gone when he went home."

Home. I remember being so struck by the word.

Certainly I knew that Nazareth was Jesus' boyhood home, but "going home" is much more a matter of the heart than a matter of distance.

Wouldn't it be wonderful, I thought, if time meant nothing and we could talk to a man who grew up with Jesus and we could listen to his stories?

I imagined such a man—not a Christian, just a boyhood friend of Jesus—who agrees to speak to us.

He might even be reluctant to begin, because he would wonder how we could possibly understand.

For this was a matter of the heart, between him . . . and 'Shua.

His real name was "Yeshua," but when I was young I couldn't say it right. I just said "'Shua," and the name caught on.

Just so you understand, I was an only child, and my mother died in childbirth. As a result, my father was a savagely bitter man. I was terrified of him. When I was small, I went looking for someone to love me. I found 'Shua.

My first memory of him was when we were six—I think it was six. It was a market day. That was always on Monday or Thursday. The farmers came into town to sell grain and sat along the wall near the well. And Miriam, 'Shua's mother, was taking him with her to buy grain. I tagged along and so did Aaron, a little runt of a kid who could always make us laugh.

Miriam went straight to her favorite dealer, a surly-faced farmer named Uriah, who had only one tooth left in all his head. I wondered why Miriam went to him. I soon found out. He took her jar, he filled it with grain, he shook it, letting it settle, and then he filled it again. The other dealers didn't do that. And he did something else.

We kids wore this linen smock that came down to our knees. Uriah pinched the front of 'Shua's smock and made a pocket and poured in more grain. A bonus! Every little bit of grain was precious to us.

Well, buying grain was also a chance for the women to share news and gossip and as a result the three of us six-year-olds got very restless. I dared 'Shua to run back across the marketplace to his house without spilling any grain. He hesitated, and I double-dared him! He clutched the grain to his chest and bolted. Aaron and I took off after him, screaming and shouting like crazy men, scattering chickens and knocking down a few toddlers. And behind me I heard the outrage of the women as they started after us.

'Shua made it to his house without dropping any grain, but then Aaron paraded around doing his imitation of Uriah with the one tooth, and we started giggling hysterically. Suddenly 'Shua began spilling the grain, which showered down over his feet. Aaron and I collapsed on the ground, shrieking with laughter and holding our stomachs. Meanwhile, the mothers advanced.

Aaron and I heard the women coming and we scrambled up and fled. But before 'Shua could move, the birds came.

Now we have more sparrows in our village than we have people, and I believe that this day there may have been every sparrow in Galilee invited to the banquet of grain on the ground.

Down they came!

At first, 'Shua tried to defend himself, holding his arms around his head. But then he became spellbound by the birds. He wandered into them and lifted his hands gently. The sparrows all rose up and hovered around him and then they came down again. 'Shua smiled and raised his hands again and they all flew up and circled around him and he started laughing with his head thrown back and spinning around watching the birds dart around his long fingers, just laughing and giggling, spinning around and around.

That's my first memory of him: dancing in ecstasy, while from all sides, doom approached.

Well, 'Shua spilled the grain, Aaron made him laugh, but it was my idea—so we were all guilty. You know how mothers think!

The punishment was left to our fathers, which meant that I spent the night in terror. When my father got through punishing me, I could barely move. I stood at my doorway in tears, holding my behind and listening to the sounds that came from 'Shua's house: "OW! . . . OW!"

For it says in Proverbs, "A man who does not discipline his son does not love him."

And we were ". . . loved."

The problem with my father was he couldn't tell the difference between discipline and cruelty. In fact, I think it never occurred to him to see any difference at all . . . if he ever loved me at all.

I took to spending more and more time at 'Shua's house and visiting with him and thinking of his parents as my own. I became "little brother," and after a while, that's what I called 'Shua—my brother.

Our village was in a bowl in the hills. 'Shua loved to run up and down those hills, as often as he could. I'd be sitting in the square and he'd go tearing through and I'd say: "Where ya goin', 'Shua?"

He'd say "C'mon, come with me," and then together we'd scramble up the stony, steep path that led between the houses, dodging garbage and debris and what we used to call "stinky stuff." Climbing up to air and freedom.

He was tall and skinny and his long legs would take him up faster than mine, and I'd have to say "Wait! Wait for me!"

And he'd say, "Oh, c'mon!" But he'd wait. And then we'd go up together.

One time—it could have been one of many—my father was enraged at me for something. After he had given me the usual beating, he shook me by the hair so badly I begged him to stop and he threw me bodily out of the house. I sat in the square, crying my eyes out in shame and humiliation. 'Shua came by and he saw me. I had bitten through my lip, and I saw him staring at it.

"Where ya goin', 'Shua?" I whimpered, my tears choking my voice. "Where ya goin'?"

"C'mon," he said, and together we went up to the hills. We sat on our favorite rocky ledge overlooking the Plain of Esdraelon, and he let me tell him all about my father and me. He put his arm around me and he let me cry and we sat. After a while, we talked about all the famous battles that had been fought on the plain below.

The day wore on, but we just sat and swung our legs and talked, and—for a time at least—everything was all right.

Those became code words between me and my brother. Whenever I needed him, all I had to say was "Where ya goin', 'Shua?" and he'd understand—especially if there were other kids around. And there were always other kids around.

Our circle of friends included 'Shua's cousins (but everybody was a cousin): Jude and James and Joses, the hyper-active, and Aaron of the wonderful humor, Reuben, a big, aggressive boy, and Eleazar—Elie—whom 'Shua loved most of all.

We played all our games together— wonderful games of football with an old goat-skin ball that was at least as old as Esau. We played pretend games like "Moses in the Wilderness" and "Joshua at Jericho," pretend wedding, pretend funeral . . .

Pretend funeral: you could be a wailer or a member of the family or the rabbi or the body. The body was an important role, but boring.

'Shua was awful as rabbi. He couldn't get out the words of commendation. He'd see one of us lying there as the body and get all choked up. And that would be it! We'd say, "Oh, 'Shua, it's just pretend," but it was no use.

I remember once when Elie was the body. He said, "'Shua, I should be in the ground by now!"

I wasn't surprised. I'd seen 'Shua weep over dead birds, and once, when the men of the village stoned to death a rabid dog in our square, he went into an alleyway and sobbed.

When he was small—and this might surprise you—he had a stutter.

I don't remember that we made much of it, but when we went to synagogue school and started learning the Scriptures in earnest, the stutter got worse and it caused him endless anguish and embarrassment.

Rabbi Mordecai ben Ezra, a lion of a man, used the repeat method to teach. He would say the lines of Scripture at the top of his voice, and we'd repeat after him at the top of ours.

"It is mercy I desire . . ." roared the rabbi.

"IT IS MERCY I DESIRE . . ." we chorused.

"And not sacrifices!"

"AND NOT SACRIFICES," we piped.

And we'd sway. Because you could physically enter the words of the Lord God, blessed be He: "It is mercy I desire . . ."

Rabbi Mordecai was more than a bit anti-Temple. He believed that we in the countryside were the real Israel—not those up in Jerusalem.

So we kept following his tune: "It is mercy I desire . . ."

"IT IS MERCY I DESIRE . . ."

But for 'Shua, words had become merciless enemies.

I'd hear him next to me: "It is . . . m . . . mercy . . . I . . . d-d-desire . . . and . . . and . . ."

Then he'd hear himself and get upset and the stammer would get worse. The kids would make fun of him until cut dead by the rabbi's stare. And I got in more than my share of fights defending my brother's pride.

Little did I realize that the fights had just begun.

There was an old woman who lived in a shack two miles out of town. She couldn't come into town because she was a public sinner—a prostitute. She was dying, anyway.

Like so many old whores, she was out of money and she was starving to death.

Well, we all knew this, but shock turned into outrage when word went around that 'Shua had taken the fish that his mother had prepared for Sabbath and given it to the whore. A Jewish boy! At a prostitute's house! With a gift! Tongues wagged, people held their heads. I wanted to defend my brother, but I was embarrassed to tears.

Rabbi Mordecai advanced on 'Shua's house with half the town.

"Spawn of Edom, come out of there!"

'Shua came out, along with his parents, who looked shaken. 'Shua was pale, and stuttering badly.

"What? What's that you say?" asked the rabbi.

"It is m-mercy . . . I-I d-desire . . . and n . . . n . . . not . . . sacrifices."

The rabbi looked startled a moment, then he reached out and grabbed 'Shua by the ear, and every kid there winced.

He said, "Maggot of Philistia, don't you realize what you have done by your unclean act? Made yourself unclean! One of my students! Unclean!"

He paraded 'Shua off toward the ritual baths, down by the well. All the kids followed, shouting things like "Get him clean, Rabbi!" "Wash him up good, Rabbi!" "Teach him a lesson, Rabbi!"

Suddenly the rabbi turned on them and said: "And is the old lady to starve, then?"

Reuben, who always resented 'Shua's leadership, yelled: "Punishment for her sins, Rabbi! Punishment for her sins!"

"And what punishment is there," hissed the rabbi, "for sins of presumption?"

Reuben wisely said nothing and just glared. And Rabbi Mordecai ben Ezra and his student Yeshua bar Joseph marched off to the ritual baths.

By the time of his bar-mitzvah, the people in my village regarded my brother as a nice boy, but distinctly odd, and punished by God with a stammer for some present or past sin. His reading at bar-mitzvah was a disaster. He couldn't get through his own chosen passage from Isaiah: "The s-spirit . . . of . . . of . . . of the L-Lord is . . . upon . . . m-me . . ."

People were polite, Reuben was smug, Elie and I died a thousand deaths for him.

In honor of his coming of age, his parents took him to Jerusalem, where for three days he tried to talk to the scribes and ask them questions. Of course, they couldn't understand a thing he said and ran out of patience, as did his parents, who couldn't find him.

My village is a big clan, that's all it is, and when 'Shua came home, his relatives were upset and angry at the way he had treated his parents. I remember I was sitting in the square and I watched 'Shua go by with his head down. To tease him, I said: "Where ya goin', 'Shua?"

He didn't look at me. He just kept his head down and practically ran up the slope to the rocky ledge. I followed him. When I stood next to him on the ledge, I saw that his face was covered with tears.

I said, "What's wrong, 'Shua?"

He turned away.

I said, "C'mon," and touched his shoulder.

He pushed my hand away.

Well, I didn't know what to do, but finally I said, "You can talk to me. I'm your brother."

He looked at me and clenched his fists. "I . . . I . . . c-can't t-t-talk to anybody," he stammered. "I c-can't . . . I c-can't . . . I can't find the . . . w-words . . . and nobody l-listens to m-m-me. Nobody listens to anything I s-s-say."

Then he threw back his head and he shrieked so loudly that it echoed off the hills: "W-WHAT'S . . . W-WHAT'S WRONG WITH ME?"

There is a time for words, and there's a time to be far from words. I just put my arm around him and got him to sit down, and after a while he let out all his grief. And it was good for him.

It was good for me, too, because little brother finally got to return some favors.

'Shua was put to the test a few
days later. It was late afternoon and all of us
boys were hot and bored. Reuben was spoil-
ing for a fight.

We were sitting in the village square when
Reuben called out, "Hey, 'Shua. How come you
got lost up in Jerusalem, huh?"

'Shua was sitting the way he always liked
to sit when he was distracted: one leg under
him, one leg straight out, and drawing with
his finger in the dirt; making circles and non-
sense things, scribbling absently in the dust.
The scribbling continued now.

"Hey, stupid," Reuben yelled, "I'm talking
to you."

Elie said, "Leave him alone!"

"Yeah, Elie," Reuben said, "defend him. Go on, defend him. You're always defending him. Let him talk for himself—if you call what he does talking. Hey, dummy, you forget you had parents?"

The scribbling stopped.

"What is it, 'Shua," Reuben sneered, "you want to be a scribe?" And he laughed.

'Shua looked at him with this absurd look of delight and said, "M-Maybe!"

And we all stared at him.

We had about as much chance of being a scribe as we did of becoming Tiberius Caesar. Even Reuben was so astounded he gave up.

At least 'Shua dreams, I thought. That's more than the rest of us do. At least he dreams.

And now I think . . . what good are dreams?

I wanted to be a carpenter like Joseph and 'Shua, and not a weaver like my father. So my father publicly disowned me and threw my belongings into the street. I was not yet sixteen.

It was all right. It was the end of things.

When my father died later that year, I had no tears for him. I had used them all up just being his son.

Joseph took pity on me and trained me in the art of carpentry, along with his own son. 'Shua and I went out and cut the trees, hauled in the logs, and threw them up onto the supports so we could saw them into planks. 'Shua mastered the bow lathe to carve furniture. I made oxen yokes and farm plows, doorways, cabinet frames—all the larger stuff.

My hands bled and blistered and I didn't care. I loved it, for I loved being with 'Shua. I would sleep on the roof of the house, and he'd come up and sleep there with me. Sometimes we'd just sit in the moonlight and talk— talk about our work, about Israel . . . about girls. We shared our ambitions. We'd pray together, we'd talk about Scripture, or we'd just lie there and count the stars, like Abraham. I do remember one titanic, Olympian wrestling match. And I almost had him! Except we rained a storm of dirt down into the house. I remember, because Joseph came up the stairs and gave us . . . an opinion about it.

When we were eighteen, we went to Sepphoris to work. Herod Antipas decided to rebuild the town, and the call went out for construction workers. So the eight of us who had grown up together, we all went. It was just four miles. The pay was good. We made new friends—even among the Gentile workers. We learned some Latin and Greek.

We were young and we were alive and it was good.

We walked back and forth to Sepphoris every day, unless the job the next day was demanding and hard and we had to get an early start. Then we would camp out at Sepphoris behind the house of Elie's cousins, Simon and Joshua. Simon was a small wiry man with intense eyes. We heard he was a zealot. We hardly ever saw him. But Joshua would sit with us every night. He was a big, friendly boy of fourteen—a carpenter, like 'Shua and me.

We'd have wonderful, passionate arguments and discussions around that fire, often ending in fights. Aaron would say something like, "The trouble with us Jews is, we have no feelings about anything." Then suddenly two of us would be rolling around on the ground trying to settle the issue!

We knew we were the remnant of Israel. We knew that the kingdom would be born. But would it be in our time? Would we see it? The Romans, of course, were a punishment for our sins. But the occupation wouldn't last forever—and after that, would Israel be restored?

We wept about it, we dreamt about it, we argued about it. We prayed: "Let it be in our time!"

What happened instead, was terrible beyond words.

And it changed our lives.

It was Friday—the day before Sabbath. Word came that an attempt had been made on the life of the Roman prefect as he rode from Caesarea by the sea up to Jerusalem.

In a rage, the Romans raided Sepphoris—which they had burned to the ground sixteen years before—and they captured ten men that they said were zealots.

They came to Simon's house, and not finding him they took his brother, Joshua. They also took the wooden supports, the poles that held up the logs so that we could saw them, and dragged all of it down the road toward the valley. There they crucified the zealots, and Joshua with them. They nailed him to his own wood and put a sign over him: "Simon did this." As the sun set for Sabbath, the victims remained on the crosses, screaming and cursing, guarded and mocked by the Romans.

For us that night, there were no joyful songs of Sabbath. There was only one song: "My God, my God, why have you abandoned me?" Elie sang, and rocked, and wept for his cousin, and when he couldn't go on, 'Shua finished the song for him.

Joshua was fourteen! Grown men could not endure the horrors of crucifixion, and Joshua was but a boy. I had heard of Roman cruelty, but this was an animal act!

Just before dawn, I heard 'Shua get up. I opened my eyes. He was taking his water-skin and putting his cloak on.

I said, "Where are you going, 'Shua?"

He held out the water-skin to me. He said, "Joshua needs us. Come with me."

"But he's got to be dead by now, 'Shua," I said. "We can't help him."

'Shua started to move off, and I caught him.

"'Shua," I said, "you can't. It's Sabbath."

"Go back to sleep, then," he said quietly, and he went out into the darkness.

I was frantic. What if 'Shua got hurt? But it was clear about Sabbath: nothing needless should be done, and this was needless! We could do nothing for the boy.

But I took my cloak, and I went. So do we make decisions in a moment, and regret them for the rest of our lives.

When we came to the crosses, it was just dawn. The Romans were gone, and only a few of the crucified were still alive. They were pulling themselves up on the nails trying to breathe, and then screaming in agony and falling back. Their voices were thick and raspy, with thirst like an axe at their throats. And everywhere there were flies—huge, black flies—covering the victims and biting into their wounds.

When we came to Joshua, he was hanging only a foot above us. His head was down on his chest, his lips were drawn back from his teeth. He was staring at us, as the flies crawled around his face.

'Shua gave him water, but it was no use. He was dead. The water dribbled out of his mouth and fell down on his chest. The flies pounced on it.

Suddenly I saw movement down the road.

Someone was riding toward us. It was a centurion. He saw us.

"'Shua," I said, "come on. It's useless. Come on. Let's go!"

'Shua pushed away my arm. He turned around and faced the soldier as he rode up. As the horse came close 'Shua lunged at it and grabbed the reins and started shouting: "*Lama? Lama? Why? Why?*"

The horse reared up, screaming. The Roman's cape kept billowing out behind him. I remember thinking, "It's red. It's red like all the blood."

Then I saw the Roman reaching for his sword. I only had time to cry "'Shua!" and the soldier slammed the haft end into my brother's head.

The next thing I remember, I was sitting in the dirt road, holding my brother's body in my arms. He was bleeding from the nose and from the ears. His blood covered my hands. In the stillness of the morning, I heard only an occasional scream from the crosses and the drone of the flies. I sat there with my brother, and wept, and kissed him, and stared at his blood on my hands.

Then I looked up. The Roman sat on his horse looking down at me, and he was smiling.

And I understood.

The Romans stripped their victims because they knew we are a modest people. They crucified us on the eve of Sabbath because they knew we are religious. And now the Roman smiled because he knew my country was his. This moment was his. Everything I cared about was his.

And he knew that I knew it.

And he smiled.

Then he turned his horse around and rode off.

With the help of two Greeks who came by whom I knew from work, I got 'Shua back to our camp, and so back home.

He lay in a coma for five days. Only his shallow breathing told us he was alive at all. His mother wept over him and bathed him. I held his hand and kept squeezing it. Elie kept talking to him in case he could hear us. Joseph sat at his son's feet, his shawl over his head, and prayed: "I have watered my bed with my tears, O my God. I have become like those who go down into the country of the dead. But you will rescue my soul. Into your hands, I commend my spirit."

On the fifth day, 'Shua opened his eyes. In a short time, he was able to eat and move around.

But then, whatever sympathy there was for us led to arguments and confusion in the village. As far as many people were concerned, 'Shua and I had broken Sabbath.

Our act of "mercy" was seen as futile—and worse—faithless.

Rabbi Mordecai came to see 'Shua. After he inquired about my brother's health, the rabbi stood looking out the doorway into the square. The wind gently lifted the fringes of his cloak. Suddenly he seemed old to me, and frail.

"I have tried," he said, "to teach as the Lord God—blest be He—has given me light. Not only Torah have I taught, but what is the heart of Torah." His voice now took on its former strength. "Not the innovations of the Pharisee or the politics of the Sadducee, no! I have taught what is essential, what all of them have never possessed: passion, commitment, the total gift of the self to the Holy One and to His Word! TOTAL!" The rabbi shouted the word.

Now as he turned toward 'Shua, his voice and manner were forlorn.

"Yeshua, did I not love Joshua as well as you? Would I not have given my own life to keep the nails from his body?"

The rabbi's eyes filled with tears.

"One day was given to us by the Lord God—blest be He," he whispered. "One day on which we can say 'He is Lord, He alone.' We cannot undo all the pain, all the suffering, all the death. We are not masters of the universe. He is Lord, and we are not! We are not! And you, Yeshua bar Joseph, you could not give him this one day?"

'Shua came over and put his hands on the rabbi's shoulders. He said: "And is . . . the o-old l-lady to s-s-starve, then?"

The rabbi shuddered. "That was different, Yeshua!"

"N-No, father," 'Shua said, "n-no. You t-taught . . . me well."

And he kissed him.

A few days later, the eight of us who worked in Sepphoris were sitting around the fire again. Reuben was breaking sticks, throwing them on a line into the flames.

"The one thing that we have," he said, looking directly at 'Shua and me, "is to be a Jew. The one thing that keeps us from the filth of the nations and the degradations of the Gentiles is to be a Jew. Our most precious possession . . . and some would betray even that."

Nobody said anything, not even Elie. There was a terrible silence.

Then 'Shua got up and came closer to the fire and he said: "The d-day we w-went to the crosses, I-I s-saw a m-man. He was l-leading his oxen to w-water. It w-was S-Sabbath, but I . . . understood."

"Understood what?" Reuben said. "Get to the point!"

'Shua whirled around, reached down, grabbed Reuben by his tunic, hoisted him to his feet and shouted in his face: "The p-point . . . is . . . a man c-can g-give his c-cattle w-what they n-n-need on S-Sabbath, b-b-but I c-can't g-give . . . a b-boy . . . on a c-cross . . . a d-drink . . . of w-water?"

Reuben gaped at him, and I think 'Shua must have seen the fear in Reuben's eyes, because he opened his hands and stepped back. Then he saw us all staring at him, and he went back and sat down next to me.

No one spoke. What was there to say?

Just before we went to sleep, 'Shua said to me, "I n-never th-thanked you e-enough for w-what you d-did for m-me. A m-man can have . . . n-no greater l-love."

"I broke Sabbath, 'Shua," I said to him.

"D-Do you th-think s-so?" he said.

Yes. I do.

I did then. I do now.

I regret that night with all my soul. The only good that came from it was this: I saw the Roman without his mask. I saw the face of the beast.

You know how it is when you love someone and it starts to go wrong? And you pretend it isn't happening?

Nothing was the same for the eight of us in the years after Joshua's death. Life took its natural course for most of us with marriage and raising families, but as we got older the bond of our youthful days was weakened. Every night all the men would go into the synagogue in Nazareth to discuss the Scriptures and to pray. But the discussions often ended in anger. Our prayer became tense and uneasy.

Aaron, for example, seemed more and more restless, as if he didn't enjoy being with us any more. His wonderful humor turned bitter. We all worried about him.

But more often than not, it was 'Shua who caused the trouble. Night after night, I watched my brother drift away from us.

I remember one night—this would be typical—we were discussing the coming kingdom of Israel. Israel restored! Rabbi Isaac, who had come to the village when Rabbi Mordecai had died, seemed to dislike 'Shua intensely. "You are not to learn Torah," the rabbi told us. "You are not to be students of the law. You are to be sons of Torah. You are to live it, to breathe it, to *be* Torah! When you are so, you will sanctify the Name, and the kingdom will come."

"Th-there is . . . m-more we have to do," 'Shua replied. "We m-must . . . t-teach those who d-do n-not know T-Torah. We m-must . . . r-rescue . . . th-the outcasts, b-because th-they have n-no one."

"It is not your job to teach, Yeshua bar Joseph," said the rabbi. "Your calling is to live Torah. They have Moses, they have the prophets—just as we do. Let them learn."

"'Shua," Jude said, trying to make peace, "does not the prophet say that in the day of the kingdom the Holy One will write His Law in our hearts, and there will be no need for teachers?"

"N-No," 'Shua said.

No. Just like that! You could feel the anger mount around him.

"N-No, w-we are to b-be what Isaiah s-said w-we are to b-be: th-the s-servants of all. W-we are t-to open the . . . eyes of the b-blind. W-we are t-to un-unstop the ears of the d-deaf. W-we are to t-tend . . . th-those . . . who n-need us."

"What about the Romans?" Reuben asked mockingly. "Shall we open their eyes, too, 'Shua? Shall we unstop their ears? Do we 'tend' the Romans, 'Shua?"

"I d-don't know," said 'Shua.

I don't . . . know.

At those words, every man who had been listening to him walked out of the synagogue, except for Elie and myself.

When they had left, Elie stooped down and picked up a handful of dirt and held it up in front of 'Shua and said: "Have you forgotten what the Romans thought of Joshua, 'Shua? That's what they think of all of us."

"Elie," 'Shua said, "I-I have t-to . . . to . . . speak the t-truth as I-I s-see it. Are you . . . afraid t-to hear the t-truth?"

Elie looked right into his eyes.

"I'm not afraid to hear it because it's true, 'Shua. I'm afraid to hear it because I love you, and you're tearing us apart!"

"Elie . . ." 'Shua said.

"No!" Elie put his hand over 'Shua's mouth. "No, 'Shua, please. No more! Peace!" He held 'Shua's face between his hands. "Shalom, Yeshua bar Joseph. No more."

Elie left. 'Shua and I sat in silence.

No more.

There was more. We heard that Aaron had stolen money from his father, called him an impotent fool, and gone away to live in Tiberias with the Gentiles. By my own beliefs I now had to regard Aaron—my dear childhood friend—as dead.

Then news came about a reformer named John the Baptizer. All of us were excited because we thought this man might signal the beginning of the kingdom. Several men of our village went down to see him and to find out what he was saying. They came back impressed, and more dedicated than ever to Torah.

'Shua went down to see John . . . and he stayed away a year.

His parents seemed to accept his absence with serenity, but I saw his mother barely survive a serious illness and his father trying to do the work of two men. I was the one who heard the criticism in the shop, in the marketplace, in the synagogue, leading me once to shout: "What are you asking me for? How am I supposed to know about him?"

And feeling ashamed.

Then it happened. I was out in the countryside on a job and Joseph was working with a boy apprentice. The support poles cracked and the logs Joseph was cutting fell on him. He lingered only a day and then he died. That just man was mourned by his wife, by his cousins, by his many friends . . . and by me.

But every eye and tongue said: "Where is his son?"

One day, months later, we were sitting in the marketplace after work. We saw a figure appear by the well road: a tall man, rather thin, his face burned black by the sun. I gasped.

'Shua.

As he strode right up to us, we all stood and stared at him in silence. He gave us the full, solemn greeting: the three kisses, holding each of us a moment with his eyes . . . Elie and me the longest.

Then he said in a voice we had never heard from him: "Brothers, the kingdom of God that we have sought for so long . . . it's come. The kingdom of God is within you!"

No trace of a stammer. Every word clear and strong.

He has found his words, I thought. And none of them makes sense.

Elie finally said to him with some sadness: "'Shua, where have you been? Your mother . . ."

"Elie!" 'Shua said, and he took him by the shoulders. "Come with me, Elie. We'll tell all of Galilee. All of Galilee should know the news."

He looked at us with pathetic eagerness. "You'll all come with me! We'll tell them together!"

"'Shua," Reuben said without a hint of compassion, "go home. Your mother is a widow."

That was cruel. But at least it was real!

'Shua looked over to the doorway of his house. His mother was standing there. He went to her and she took him in her arms.

I went with them to Joseph's grave. 'Shua threw himself on the ground and sobbed. I wanted to scream at him: where were you? Why weren't you here when we needed you?

Yet three days later, 'Shua held *shiva* for a total stranger!

A tax collector, living in the same shack where the old whore had lived, died. 'Shua heard about it, went out, and buried the man. And he held *shiva* for him—as if anyone would come to comfort someone over the death of a leech! Yet 'Shua threw dirt on his head and wailed for the man as if he cared about him. Then he refused to bathe after making himself unclean and forced everyone to avoid him.

Shortly after that scandal, the Romans came to our village "requisitioning." That's their word for robbing us of food. We stood on the sides of the square in utter silence and just watched them—the way you watch insects in the dirt.

'Shua, though, walked out to an auxiliary who was standing in the middle of the square and offered him bread. Family food! The sign of brotherhood!

The auxiliary didn't know what to do. Before he could do anything, however, the centurion rode over and said: "Don't eat that. This rat may have put poison in it."

You see, they don't think we know any Greek, and they don't think we know their little joke—that Romans think Jews look like the sewer rats of Rome.

'Shua knew what the soldier said, so he broke the bread in half, bit off a portion from each side, and held it out to both of them.

The centurion said: "He's crazy. Let's get out of here."

When the Romans had gone, Elie walked up to 'Shua and said in a voice that was barely audible: "Who are you? Where's my friend? He left here, you know, and was gone a long time and never came back. What did you do with him?"

"Elie," 'Shua said, "the kingdom is here. The hatred must end."

Elie spat full in his face.

This is never, ever done among us—and never to a brother, no matter what the cause. I know Elie was sorry for it instantly, because after a moment he reached out and gently wiped the spittle from 'Shua's face.

Then he turned and left the square.

"Elie!" 'Shua cried. "Elie!"

But Elie didn't come back. Nor did anyone, for they had all left the square. 'Shua dropped the bread into the dirt and just stood there, tears coming down his face.

For some reason, I knew he would be up on our special ledge that night, and I went to reason with him. But I didn't, because when I got up to the ledge, I heard 'Shua moaning: "Abba . . . Abba . . . Abba . . ."

"Father . . ."

Now he mourns for Joseph, I thought. Now, when it's too late.

His last day with us was a market day. 'Shua was sitting outside his house. The market was in full turmoil as usual, but people were avoiding his side of the square. I was sitting by the well. 'Shua was looking at every person and thing as if he had never seen them before. His eyes lingered on people, the animals, the shop wares. Then I felt his eyes come to me. He looked at me a long time.

But I couldn't look at him.

Suddenly, there was a silence in the square. I looked to my left. It was Aaron. He was filthy, dressed in Gentile rags. His face was gaunt and bore the marks of disease. He was looking across the square to his father and his brother, who were staring back at him in disbelief.

"Father," Aaron called, "I have sinned against heaven and against you. I am not worthy to be called your son. But please, father . . . let me come home. Please."

Aaron's father shook with emotion and said: "I had a boy like you once, but . . . he . . . got . . . lost. I had a younger son, but . . . he . . . died." The old man turned and left the square.

Aaron ran to his brother and clutched his arm: "Please, brother, intercede for me. You must!"

The brother said with disdain, "How can I be a brother . . . to a Gentile and a thief?"

He shook off Aaron's hand and walked away.

Well, you know what happened, don't you? Of course you do! 'Shua went up to Aaron, embraced him, and said: "You can stay at my house."

Reuben shouted across the whole square: "That's right, 'Shua. Take him in. Trash belongs with trash, garbage with garbage!"

To give Aaron his due, he shook his head and said: "No, 'Shua, no. I will not bring shame on your family."

Then Aaron turned away and slowly trudged back down the road he had come.

"Shame?" 'Shua cried after him. "What shame that isn't here already?"

"Family?" He looked at all of us, his eyes wide with anger. "I HAVE NO FAMILY!"

A short while later, he left us.

The next thing we heard of 'Shua, he was in Capernaum. He was preaching and healing and he was forgiving sins. 'Shua? Forgiving sins? The group following him was more deluded than he was. They called him the Messiah!

Messiah? A carpenter from Nazareth? They never came to ask us. No one came to us! It was madness!

His mother and I and some of his other relatives went down to talk to him—just to talk some sense. His "disciples" told him his family was there, and 'Shua looked at the scum he was sitting with and said: "Here is my family. Here's my mother, my sister . . . my brother."

'Shua said that to our faces!

Oh, he came home—once!—and there was violence in the synagogue. You can only insult what is precious to people so long before they'll strike back.

And when he took his insane parade to Jerusalem and they crucified him, you will understand if I say . . . we were *not* surprised!

I . . . didn't mean to sound harsh . . . when I said that . . . I don't mean to sound cruel. I've described crucifixion to you. No one should have to die that way. No one.

It's just that 'Shua should have known . . .

He . . . should've . . .

Do you know what hurts so much in all this?

It wasn't me—or my people—who deserted him when he was in need. We weren't the ones who left him all alone to face his enemies. We weren't the ones who finally broke his heart.

It was all those he cared for who did that.

My brother gave them everything he had, even . . . even the love he used to give me.

And it meant *nothing* to them!

That's what hurts. It hurts so bad.

Because I still see him. Over and over I see him. He's standing there and he's holding that water-skin and he's saying to me, "C'mon. Come with me."

And I'm saying, "Where ya goin',
'Shua?"

"Where ya goin'?"